THE PAINTED GARDEN
A year in words and watercolours
by Mary Woodin

RUNNING PRESS
Philadelphia · London

Printed in China

9 8 7 6 5 4 3 2 1

Digit on the right indicates the number of this printing.
Library of Congress Cataloging-in-Publication Number
98-066650
ISBN 0-7624-1530-4

Art Direction by Ken Newbaker
Edited by Caroline Tiger
Cover Design by Bill Jones

This book may be ordered by mail from the publisher.
Please include $2.50 for postage and handling.
BUT TRY YOUR BOOKSTORE FIRST!
Running Press Book Publishers
125 South Twenty-second Street
Philadelphia, Pennsylvania 19103-4399.

Visit us on the web!
www.runningpress.com

For my family

Contents

July.

the herb garden

in midsummer

August. Keeping the garden in trim.

September. Warm tones of late summer

October. First leaves are turning

November.

Berries and birdsong.

December.

A celebration of evergreens

Foreword.

The idea for this book arose out of my two greatest passions — it is an artist's and a gardener's journal. I have spent a glorious year, paintbrush in one hand, trowel in the other, recording the comings and goings in my garden. from bulbs and blossom, to birds and a baby!

I live in Blackheath, a delightfully leafy suburb of London, with my husband Andrew, daughter Saskia and baby Reuben, who entered the scene halfway through this year.

In the 1830s our georgian house was surrounded by fourteen acres of hayfields, green lawns and a boating lake. Sadly no more. Now we content ourselves with being surrounded by birdsong and enough garden to grow my favourite flowers.

I studied at the Royal College of Art, London, and flower painting was a discipline that was instilled in me early on. All the paintings in this journal were done in watercolour, and most of them outside in the garden.

The starting point for my garden was to grow the flowers I love to paint - irises, roses, cottage garden favourites - scabious cosmos, sweet-peas. Each plant comes with its own history —

some I've nurtured lovingly from seed. Rarely can I resist a purchase at the nursery of a memorable garden, and I can always find a space for orphans when my mother has been dividing her perennials. And so my garden grows.

"If you would be happy for a week, take a wife,
If you would be happy for a month, kill your pig,
But if you would be happy all your life — plant a garden."

CHINESE PROVERB

"To me the meanest flower that blows can give
Thoughts that do often lie too deep for tears."
WORDSWORTH

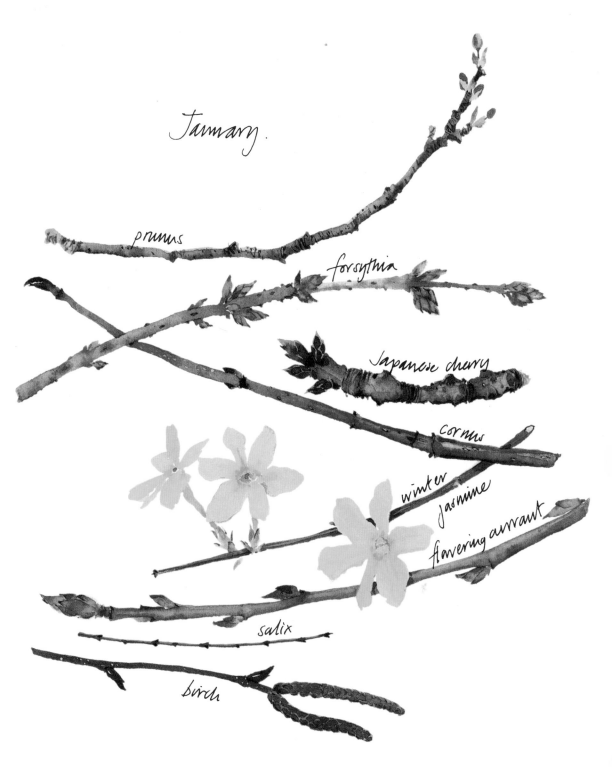

January.

prunus

forsythia

Japanese cherry

cornus

winter jasmine

flowering currant

salix

birch

The fragile first petals on the prunus

Iris reticulata

anemone blanda in the woodland garden.

periwinkle - sorcerer's violet

4th Jan. Gales and lashing rain. First disaster of the new year - my rose obelisk has been reduced to a tangle of sticks.

"Riding on the crest of a wave that tries to submerge us is one of the phases of our existence that makes life most satisfactory and worth living, and it is the secret of all progress. If gardening were easy, even under favourable circumstances, we should none of us care to do it." MRS C.W. EARLE. POT-POURRI FROM A SURREY GARDEN 1887.

Blue Tit

Great Tit.

9th Jan.
A mild day with
sunny spells. The
blue-tits are pirouetting in
the forsythia. I put up some
feeders for them, but have
failed in my attempts to
make them squirrel proof.
The blackbirds and thrushes
swoop down on the apple
peelings left out for them.
13th Jan. St Hilary's Day —
the coldest day of the year.
The camellia buds are already
fat and flushed with pink.

"A Gard'ner's work is never at an end; it begins with the Year and continues to the next." JOHN EVELYN
THE GARD'NER'S ALMANAC 1664

Primula Gold Lace

19th January. We're enjoying sunny but cold days with early morning frosts. Covered new shoots on the perennials with bracken to deter Jack Frost's icy fingers. The japonica quince is smothered with goblets of deep coral. Pale blue dwarf irises spread wide their papery tongues of pastel colour. Primulas parade their jewels of scarlet and purple.

hyacinth daffodil crocus tulip

28th Jan. A muted
grey day with mist-
like rain that lingers
on the air.

Cyclamen hederifolium

Pinks blooming on the rockery

fragrantissima

A short walk around the garden
gives a thrill almost more profound
than the generosity of summer.
Each twig closely observed is
filled with anticipation. Tiny pink
buds on the prunus, knobbly curves
on the cherry and apple, the
smooth red bark of the dogwoods.

flowering currant.

February.

" Bees come out of their hives,
the partridge begins to pair, the
blackbird whistles and the
field and woodlarks
sing. "

J.C. LOUDON 1882 ENCYLLOPAEDIA OF GARDENIN

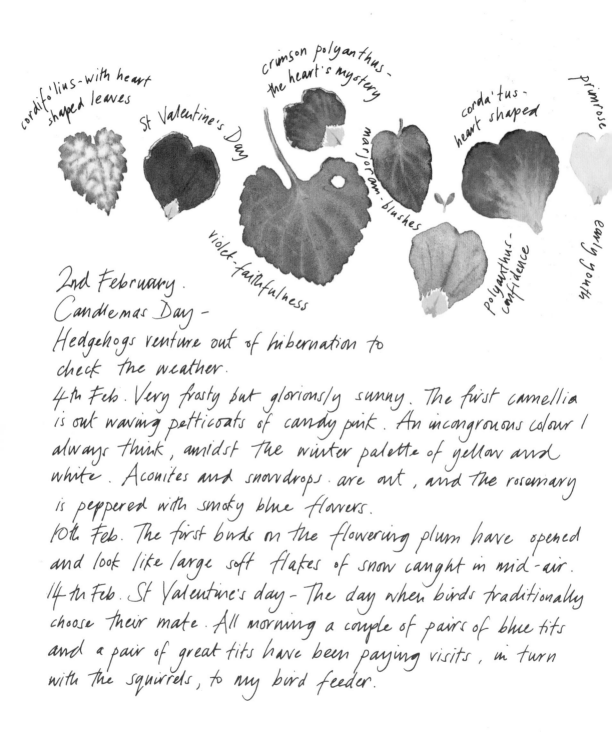

cordifo'lius - with heart shaped leaves

St Valentine's Day

crimson polyanthus - the heart's mystery

marjoram - blushes

corda'tus - heart shaped

primrose

early youth

violet - faithfulness

polyanthus - confidence

2nd February.
Candlemas Day —
Hedgehogs venture out of hibernation to
check the weather.
4th Feb. Very frosty but gloriously sunny. The first camellia
is out waving petticoats of candy pink. An incongruous colour I
always think, amidst the winter palette of yellow and
white. Aconites and snowdrops are out, and the rosemary
is peppered with smoky blue flowers.
10th Feb. The first buds on the flowering plum have opened
and look like large soft flakes of snow caught in mid-air.
14th Feb. St Valentine's day — The day when birds traditionally
choose their mate. All morning a couple of pairs of blue tits
and a pair of great tits have been paying visits, in turn
with the squirrels, to my bird feeder.

Crocus – Gipsy Girl

Grape hyacinth

Hyacinth Blue Princess

18th Feb. An unusually warm weekend has coaxed the garden into bloom – the flowering plum is smothered in white blossom. The crocuses which have stood tightly budded for several days, flaunt their petals in the sun. Plant them near lavender to stop the birds pecking the petals.

snowdrop

hyacinth

daffodil

muscari

chinodoxa

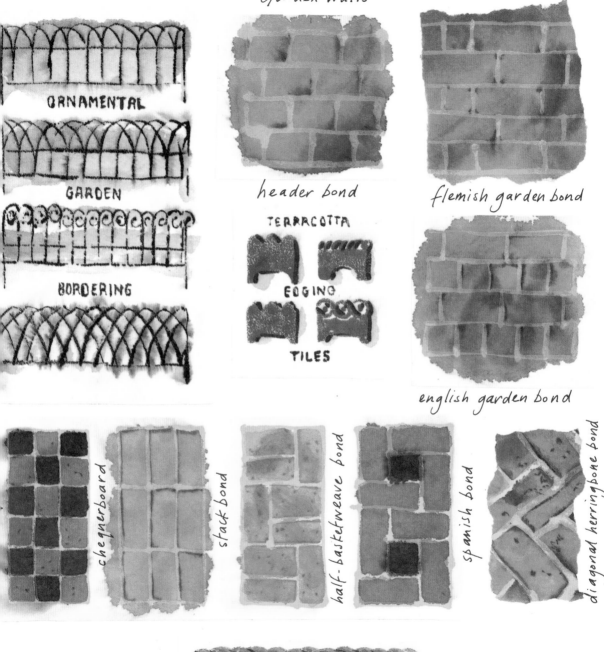

Garden walls

ORNAMENTAL

GARDEN

BORDERING

header bond

flemish garden bond

TERRACOTTA

EDGING

TILES

english garden bond

chequerboard

stack bond

half-basketweave bond

spanish bond

diagonal herringbone bond

gravel

CABLE PATTERN

Each time I wander round the garden, new shoots and flowers have appeared - often a long forgotten flower that quite surprises me, like a clump of dwarf narcissi that stays quite hidden in the grape hyacinths until their heads are quite swollen and ready to burst.

"Half the interest of a garden is the constant exercise of the imagination. You are always living three or indeed six months hence. I believe that people entirely devoid of imagination never can be really good gardeners. To be content with the present, and not striving about the future is fatal."

MRS C.W. EARLE. POT-POURRI FROM A SURREY GARDEN 1887

aubrieta.
lily of the valley
violets
grape hyacinth.
dwarf narcissi
pinks.
violas
primroses

24th St Matthias's Day

'St Mathee sends
The sap up the tree.'

27th February.
The forsythia buds that the birds
haven't stripped are now showing
quite yellow, and the wintersweet
is out around the pond.
The rhubarb is pushing its first
crumpled leaves through the strawy
manure that covers it. Place dark
heavy pots over, to force the tender
pink shoots.
28th Feb. Dug out a new south-
facing border in the back garden.
Picked out bucketfuls of stones to use
as drainage at the bottom of pots.
Pruned the roses. The pink climber
has not stopped flowering all winter.

forcing rhubarb.

"Crocuses – Protect from birds by running a small piece of white thread or string along, six inches above the plants; thin, and almost invisible; the bird does not see it till it alights for a feast, and before proceeding to make a meal of the budding Crocus it looks up, sees the string, pipes out danger, and away it goes, and familiarity with the thread does not breed indifference, for the same process is repeated again and again, to the safety of the Crocuses; coloured string is of no use as a preventive."

THE ILLUSTRATED GUIDE FOR AMATEURS
DANIELS BROS. 1876

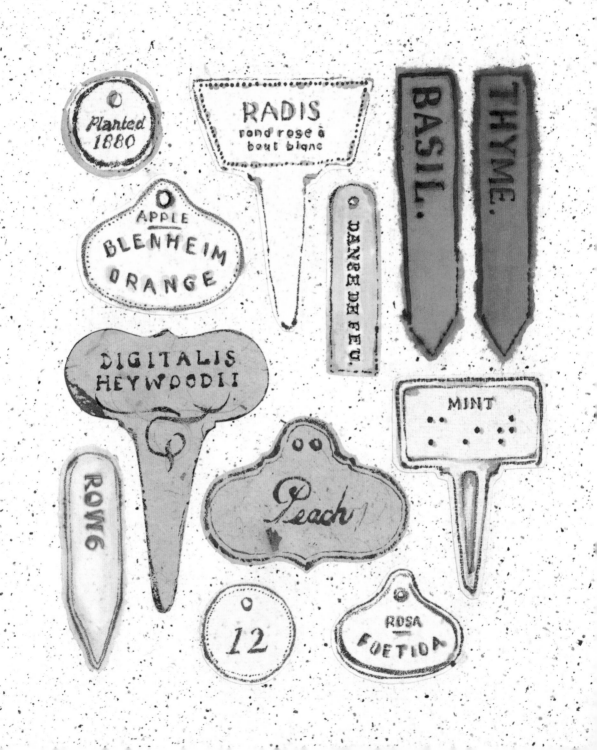

H.E.R.B.S

CHIVES
Allium schoenoprasum

12" - 15" height
prefers a
bright sunny
position
and moist
soil

TOMATO GARDENERS DELIGHT

MARJORAM (POT)
Origanum onites

Ordinary soil
Soft green leaves
purple
flowers late summer

Culinary uses

use leaves
in
stuffings with
meats
or vegetables.

HARDY PERENNIAL LUPIN
RUSSELL MIXED

SUN OR
PARTIAL
SHADE

Fragaria PINK PANDA

Ideal for border, hanging
baskets and containers

Clematis
Elsa Späth

MARCH

HELXINE BABY'S TEARS

keep soil moist

" IN MARCH AND APRILL, FROM MORNING TO NIGHT,
IN SOWING AND SETTING GOOD HUSWIVES DELIGHT. "
THOMAS TUSSER. FIVE HUNDRED POINTS OF GOOD HUSBANDRIE 1573.

Camellia japonica
'Elegans'

2nd March - Saw the first
peacock butterfly sunning
its open wings on the warm
flagstones. A huge bumble
bee is busy whirling round
the blossom. The camellias
are in full flight, bearing
extravagant blooms. The
weather continues to be so
mild, it's easy to become
complacent and forget how
damaging a late frost can be.

cottage garden mix

Plant your seeds in a row

1. for the pheasant
1. for the crow
1. to rot and
1. to grow   anon

cosmos
love in a mist
cornflower
nasturtium
sweet pea
hollyhock
aquilegia
knautia
scabiosa
candytuft

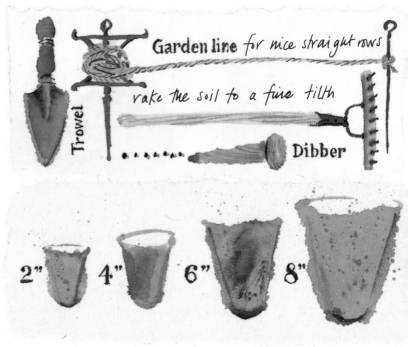

Trowel

Garden line for nice straight rows

rake the soil to a fine tilth

Dibber

2"   4"   6"   8"

carrot
cress
cauliflower
cabbage
brussels
leek
lettuce
radish
beetroot
parsnip
pea
courgette
french bean
runner bean

March 6th. Checked
seed packets for sowing
times. Sowed aquilegia
knautia and viola.
March 6. 1771. Monticello.
Sowed a patch of peas
after steeping them in
water for 24 hours.
7. rain, snow and hail
with an Easterly wind for
4 days.
25. Peas up.
May 26. The greatest flood
ever known in Virginia.
30. Peas of Mar 6 come to
table." JEFFERSON'S GARDEN BOOK 1771
Plant marigolds with potatoes
to keep pests at bay, and
sweetpeas amongst beans to
increase yield. To ensure
germination of melon seeds,
warm them before sowing —
March 15. 1755. Carry'd Mr.
Garnier's Canteleupe-seed..in
my breeches pocket 6 or 8
weeks." GILBERT WHITE

VEGETABLE SEEDS

RADISH
SCARLET WHITE - TIPPED EARLY

VEGETABLE SEEDS

CAULIFLOWER
PILGRIM (late April - May) 50 seeds

PEA - RONDO

Height 25-30 in   200 seeds

VEGETABLE SEEDS

CARROT
FLYAWAY   500 seeds

17th March. The bluebells in the dell are showing
thick tufts of bright green, and bear the promise of
swathes of heavenly blue. The ground has been
refreshed by gentle warm rains. The hardy geraniums
froth with tender new leaves.
18th Planted up a pot of nettles to put by the buddlea -
butterflies love to lay their eggs on its leaves.

meadow brown

gatekeeper

common
blue

small copper

painted lady

holly blue

speckled wood

wall brown

peacock

large white

" These butterflies in twos and threes,
That flit about in wind and sun —
see how they add their flowers to flowers,
And blossom where a plant has none ." W.H. DAVIES.

20th March. The magpies and rooks, of which we have far too many in the garden, are busy pulling moss from the lawn for their nests.

> "We have a tradition or, if you will
> a superstition, in this part of the
> world, that rooks always begin to
> build on the first Sunday in March."
> HENRY A. BRIGHT. A YEAR IN A LANCASHIRE GARDEN 1879

21st. The ground is still damp - I spent a happy afternoon weeding!

> "Here remember, that you never take
> in hand or begin the weeding of
> your beds, before the earth be made
> soft, through the store of rain falling
> a day or two before." THOMAS HYLL
> THE GARDENER'S LABYRINTH 1590

23rd The violets are out in full now, deep, velvety and fragrant. Their flowers are fairly short-lived, but I value them almost as much for their abundant heart-shaped leaves which provide good ground cover for shady corners, all year round. Growing through them, the compact heads of grape hyacinths nod silently, "as if a cluster of grapes and a hive of honey had been distilled and compressed together into one small boss of celled and beaded blue" RUSKIN.

April.

"Is any moment of the year more delightful than the present? What there is wanting in glow of colour is more than made up for in fullness of interest. Each day some well-known, long remembered plant bursts into blossom."

HENRY A. BRIGHT. A YEAR IN A LANCASHIRE GARDEN 1879

5th April - Primrose day. a mild spring has meant the primroses are long gone.

'If you'd enjoy the fruit pluck the flower' (old saying)

Mulch strawberries with pine needles for a sweeter flav[our]

Myosotis palustris - mouse ear bird's eye forget-me-not robin's eye

Dianthus

emblem of love

deep purple aubretia variegated - plant on stone wall - good butterflies.

citrus with grey green leaves

Anemone

periwink[le]

cherry blossom out

wallflower - an early flower for bees

Leopards bane - one of the first splashes of spring colour are already nearly over - a few drops of tincture of leopards bane in hot water makes a soothing footbath.

5th April. The cherry blossom through my studio windows is an explosion of pale pink. The leaves as they emerge are a soft russet brown fading gradually to sap green. The strawberries are in flower, the tiny green fruits circled by white petals. Keep them well watered as the fruits swell. The rhubarb stalks are plump enough to eat. Bake in the oven simply sprinkled with sugar and a little ginger. Serve with cream.

10th. Potted up parsley seedlings. Love-lies-bleeding seeds have germinated.

"To create a little flower is the labour of ages" WILLIAM BLAKE.

The forget-me-nots are a haze of soft blue, and the lilies-of-the-valley are slowly unfurling. Tufty yellow heads of dandelion light up the hedgerows, the bluebells are just beginning to open. Miniature speedwell flowers weave through the grass, whilst fallen hawthorn petals lace the scene.

Japanese Cherry

"In April. The Double
white Violet, The Wall-flow
The Stock-Gilly-Flower;
The Couslip;
Flower-Deli
and Lilie
of all Nat
Rose-ma
Flowers; Th
Tulippa; the
Double Piony;
The Pale Daffa
The French Honnu
Suckle; The Ch
Tree in Blosso
FRANCIS BACON

The first spring blown anemone
she in his doublet wove,
to keep him safe from pestillence
wherever he should rove.
TRAD RHYME

leather gauntlets

Blustery sunny day. Secure clematis, tie in new shoots around rose arch. Wallflowers are out.

"Most operations may be performed with common gloves. Thus, no gardener need have hands like bear's paws"

J.C.LOUDON. ENCYCLOPAEDIA OF GARDENING 1871

12th April

cotton gloves

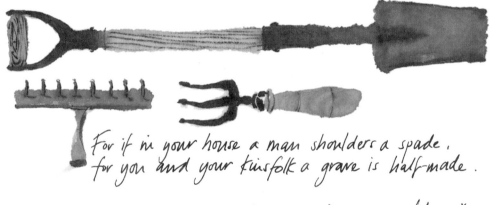

For if in your house a man shoulders a spade, for you and your kinsfolk a grave is half-made.

"Beware of all enterprises that require new clothes"
THOREAU 1854

Recipe for waterproofing boots before the invention of Wellingtons –
1 pint boiled linseed oil
½ lb mutton suet
4 oz resin
6 oz clean beeswax.
melt, mix and brush, whilst still warm, onto dry leather boots or shoes.

FRITILLARIA
MICHAILOVSKYI.

"The spring flowers I really care about are those
that come up every year in the mixed borders....
They are old friends that never fail us; they ask
only to be left alone, and are the most welcome
"harbingers of spring" bringing with them the pleasant
memories of former years, and the fresh promise of the
year that is to come." HENRY A. BRIGHT. A YEAR IN A LANCASHIRE GARDEN 1879

April 16th. We returned home last night. At this time of year how a week or ten days changes the growth in one's garden! I must confess that sometimes, coming home after dark, I have taken a hand-candle to inspect some special favourite."

MRS C.W. EARLE. POT-POURRI
FROM A SURREY GARDEN 1897

April 20th. Tulips, vida, chinodoxa, hellebore, vinca, fritillaria.

April 21st. Another trip to the plant nursery to fill in a few gaps in my new south-facing bed

"I have recently heard it advocated as a short cut to harmony that all red and scarlet flowers be banished from the garden. This, I think, would be sad indeed, for much of warmth and strength, of flash and spirit would depart with them."

LOUISE BEEBE WILDER. COLOUR IN MY GARDEN 1927

" There is lately a Flower
(shall I call it so ? in
courtesie I will tearme it
so, though it deserve not the
appellation) a Toolip, which
hath engrafted the love and
affections of most people unto
it; and what is this Toolip?
a well complexioned stink,
an ill favour wrapped up
in pleasant colours. "

THOMAS FULLER 1650

Apple - Espalier Spar

Espalier
Laxton Fortune

Grie

Malus
Red Glow

Royalty

Apricot Fan Moorpark

Simco

Morello
Cherry

Nectarine Fan
Pineapple

Fig - Fa

Apple

Ballerina bolero

"The reign of pink is inaugurated in the garden with the festival of the blossoms. We have the full-costumed Peach trees, the twisted, rose-wrapped branches of the Crab apples and many exquisite forms of pink double flowered Japanese Cherries and Plums."

LOUISE BEEBE WILDER
COLOUR IN MY GARDEN
1927

higher the plum
riper the plum

Plant pears for
your heirs

If apples bloom in March
for fruit you may search

my father's quince tree

April 26th.
Cherry, apple, pear, nectarine, apricot - I spent a lovely sunny day painting in a favourite orchard, surrounded by every shade of pink my palette could contrive. From the softest peachy pink on the bud of 'bolero', to the purple madder of malus 'royalty.'

cauliflower
snowcrown

onion set jagro

parsnip
white gem

turnip
snowball early white stone

cabbage
sown 21 January

outdoor cucumber
bush crop

main crop potato valour
planted 7 April

courgette ambassadore

sweetcorn
sunrise

beef tomato
marmande

shallot
giant long keeping yellow.

beetroot
boltardy.

brussels sprouts
f1 silverline

broad bean
jade 14.4.97

snap pea
sugar bon. sown 6 Mar.

cos lettuce
lobjoits green cos

carrot sytan
sown 17 March

dwarf french bean
masterpiece

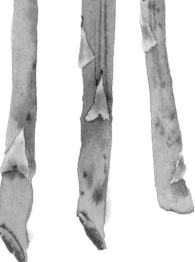

"Dig the ground three spits deep —
that is, the depth of three spades —
and put in everything you can
that is good : well-rotted farm-
manure, the emptying of cesspools,
butcher's offal, dead animals,
anything to enrich the soil for a
long time."

MRS C.W. EARLE - ON PLANTING
ASPARAGUS. "POT-POURRI FROM A SURREY GARDEN" 1887

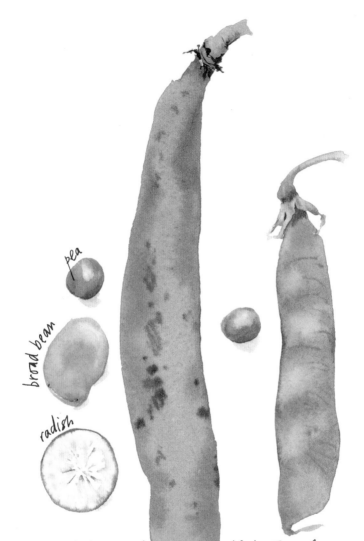

pea

broad bean

radish

"Carrets are good to be eaten with saltfish. Therefore sowe Carrets in your Gardens, and humbly praise God for them, as for a singular and great blessing; Admit if it should please God that any City or Towne should be besieged with the Enemy, what better provision for the greatest number of people can bee, then every garden to be sufficiently planted with Carrets?"

RICHARD GARDINER 1603

The beauty there is in mosses
will have to be considered from
the holiest quietest nook "
THOREAU.

chinodoxa

common bullfinch

Children who eat
primroses will see
fairies.

" The flower which
above all others yield,
the sweetest smell
the air is the violet.
BACON

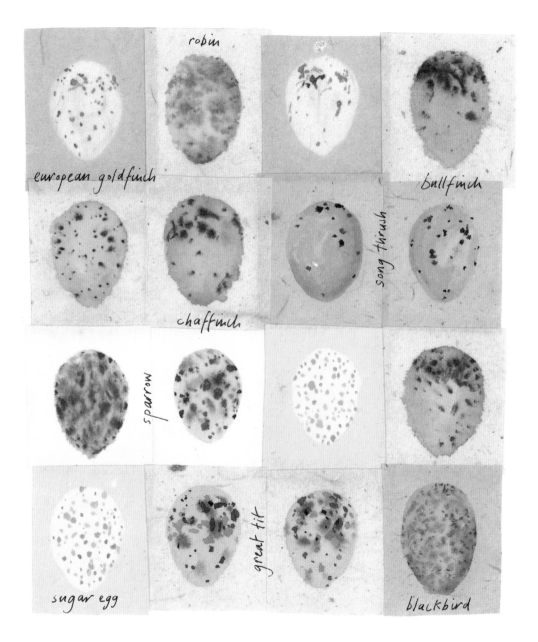

robin

european goldfinch

bullfinch

song thrush

chaffinch

sparrow

sugar egg

great tit

blackbird

May

"Man has availed himself of the great laws of evolution in mightier matters than the Iris, but in no theatre of his unsleeping efforts has he created purer beauty or wakened for flower lovers a truer joy than among the bearded Irises."

EDEN PHILLPOTT
COUNTRY LIFE MAGAZINE 1917

"Iris is soe named from the
resemblance of the rainbow in heaven
DIOSCORIDES. FIRST CENTURY A.D.

"For his excellent beautie and rarietie deserveth first place." JOHN PARKINSON 1627 (ON THE IRIS)

1st May. If I had to choose one favourite flower it would be the iris. They will very soon be out - already their tightly parceled petals are yearning to be unwrapped. The first rose is out, the sage is in flower and alive with bees. The ceanothus is a glorious swathe of powder blue, but the slugs are munching the poppies.

8th May. The week has ended with a flourish — the irises are out! The weather is still unfavourably cold, which means numb fingers and several pairs of socks whilst I'm out painting. I want to capture their stance, sometimes standing tall, other times bowing under the weight of heavy blooms. The velvety depth of their petals with their translucent ruffled edges. Colours are never harsh - purple fades to blue, yellow to gold, orange to russet. The way the bud opens, the papery casing peeling away, and the way, all too soon, those princely petals curl in on themselves to die.

The fairest flowers soonest fade TRAD. SAYING

poo on nicotiana seedlings

alkanet

dandelion

oxalis

grass

herb robert

Keep topiary in trim

Dead head flowers regularly

16th May. At last the weather has turned warmer and everything in the garden has swelled to double its size in a matter of days. Every step through the garden adds a job to the list.

- weed! "plantain - place a piece of table salt the size of a hazel nut on the very middle of the plant in hot dry weather - in two or three days the leaves will blacken and the root will completely perish" CANON ELLACOMBE IN MY VICARAGE GARDEN AND ELSEWHERE 1901.

- feed tomatoes weekly once first truss has set.

- first strawberry nearly ripe. put nets over.

- plant out spring sown sweet peas on wigwams at the corners of the rhubarb patch.

"Finish off one job before you begin another. This advice is trite, but it is of great importance, and there are few cases where it cannot be attended to." J. C. LOUDON ENCYCLOPAEDIA OF GARDENING

...flo'rus-
...sing
...ite
...wers

20th May – sunny spells, thundery
showers

au'reus – golden
yellow

...on't go to law with your neighbour,
...cause his bees suck honey from your flowers

dehis'cens –
splitting open
to scatter seeds

...s'pus-
...ted

...crispula

Nigella damascena
of Damascus, Syria

va'gans – wandering

capil'lipes –
with a slender stalk

grow nasturtiums
in poor soil to
produce more
flowers and less
leaves.

...itriodo'rus – lemon scented

Jobs aside, May is a wonderful time for making garden visits to enjoy the bounty of the month.

23rd May. The scrolled iron gate gives a melodic clang as we turn the rusty handle and step into the courtyard, the air heavy with the perfume of roses. Noisettes, Sweet briars, Hybrid Teas, Chinas. An old fashioned white climber with great glorious blooms scrambles over centuries of red brick. Creamy nasturtiums tangle at it's feet. Two stone dogs gaze faithfully on - the lichen of ages colouring their backs. A narrow gravel path leads along the golden walk - a shimmering avenue of apricot roses, lemony lupins and orange lilies. Down worn steps, past pillars and urns, at each turn the senses are besieged - a shower of mauve clematis, a curtain of white foxgloves, lupins painted in every shade of pink.

In the kitchen garden, the rhythmic scraping of a hoe echoes off the enclosing walls. Peach leaves curl against south facing brick.

silvery sage

feverfew

golden leaved marjoram

tiny variegated thyme

chives bordering the rhubarb

Behind the Victorian greenhouse, tulip bulbs dry in the midday sun. Inside, garlands of scarlet geraniums twist and twirl.

Sweet pea wigwams at the corners of the vegetable plot.

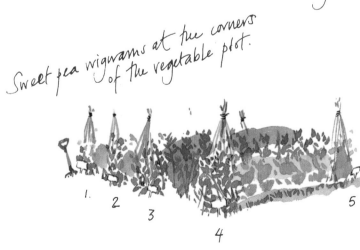

1. Captain Scott
2. Southampton.
3. Blue Triumph
4. Jasmine Kalm
5 Xenia Field

salvia nemerosa

iris

pyrethrum thomasini

astrantia graniolica

geum
Lady Stratheden

veronica sightsein

alchemilla mollis

papaver orientale
harvest moon

lupin

aquilegia McKanas
hybrid

campanula globerata
superba

kniphofia

polymonium blue pearl

geranium

potentilla recta warenni

campanula persifolia blue

aquillea filipendula
gold plate

lychnis chalcedonica

"This little space which scented box encloses
Is blue with lupins and is sweet with thyme
My garden all is overblown with roses,
My spirit is all overblown with rhyme,
As like a drunken honeybee I waver
From house to garden and again to house,
And undetermined which delight to favour,
On verse and rose alternately carouse."

VITA SACKVILLE-WEST 1917

June

" The rose doth deserve the chiefest place amongst all flowers whatsoever; being not only esteemed for its beauty, virtues and fragrant and odoriferous smell but also because it is the honour and ornament of our English sceptre."

GERARD. HERBAL 1597

English Rose Redcoat.

Rosa Essex

Rosa Suffolk

Rosa Kent

Rosa Surrey

miniature roses

June 1st. Roses are one of the most challenging
flowers to paint - to capture at once the depth,
the softness, the layers of interwoven petals, the
fragility of white or the richness of red.

"There should be beds of roses, banks of roses,
bowers of roses, hedges of roses, edgings of roses,
baskets of roses, vistas and alleys of roses."

REVD. SAMUEL REYNOLDS HOLE. A BOOK ABOUT ROSES 1869

MARY ROSE

Just Joey – Hybrid Tea

June 2nd

The first rose to flower
Rosa foetida 'Austrian Yellow'
a native from the 16th Century.

sisyrinchium

Eglantine

double geranium in a shady corner

Sage - busy with bees

"... a bank whereon the wild thyme blows
Where oxlips and the nodding violet grows
Quite over-canopied with luscious woodbine
With sweet musk-roses and with Eglantine :"

SHAKESPEARE 1594

Oak rose - flowers last
& for a day

generous and devoted affection

honeysuckle

By the steps to the
kitchen garden, the rose
arch is covered with
the pink blooms of
Eglantine. Through it
jasmine and honeysuckle
weave and wind.

consper'sus : speckled

Fragaria vesca

3rd June. The strawberries
are ripe. Legend has it, the
first strawberry should be
given to the birds, but not
until I've painted it.
Anyway, my daughter Saskia

is much quicker off the mark than the
birds when it comes to red strawberries. My
mother arrived with a basketful of redcurrants
from her garden. Made redcurrant and
mint jelly — add a handful of fresh mint
to the redcurrants whilst cooking.

4th June.
Picked herbs
for drying —
in the morning
once the dew
had evaporated.

made flavoured vinegars

THYME

RASPBERRY

BAY

REDCURRANT

Scabious - Bachelor's buttons,
Pins and Needles, Lady's cushion
Gipsy rose, Teddy buttons.

5th June.
In the abundance of
summer there are always
flowers that I do not
find time to paint - chose
some for pressing - campanula,
penstemon, papaver, aquilegia.

It's also a nice memento, to press blooms from posies given to me from friends' gardens.

7th June. The weather is unrelentingly wet. The annuals are struggling to keep their heads above water.

"7th June 1787. Ice thick as a crown piece. Potatoes much injured and whole rows of kidney beans killed; nasturtiums killed." GILBERT WHITE A NATURALISTS JOURNAL 1787

16th June. As the month progresses the pink palette of early summer is making way for the blues of midsummer.

"Blue! gentle cousin of the forest green,

Married to green in all the sweetest flowers."

KEATS

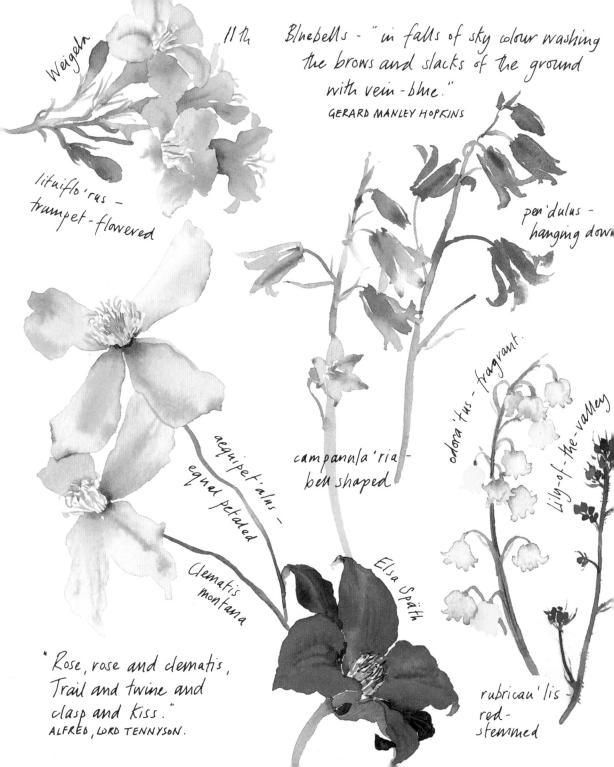

Weigela

11th

Bluebells - "in falls of sky colour washing the brows and slacks of the ground with vein-blue."
GERARD MANLEY HOPKINS

lituiflo'rus –
trumpet-flowered

pen'dulus –
hanging down

aequipet'alus –
equal petaled

campannla'ria –
bell shaped

odora'tus – fragrant.

Lily-of-the-valley

Clematis montana

Elsa Späth

"Rose, rose and clematis,
Trail and twine and
clasp and kiss."
ALFRED, LORD TENNYSON.

rubricau'lis –
red-
stemmed

" with five little hollowe hornes,
as it were hanging foorth,
with small leaves standing
upright of the shape of
little birds." GERARD.

Aquilegia vulgaris - Columbine
or . . . .
   Granny's bonnet,
     Lady's slippers,
Doves in the Ark,
    Fool's cap,
      Hen and chickens.

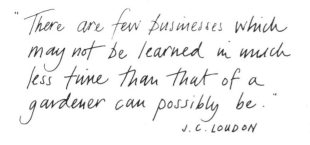

"There are few businesses which may not be learned in much less time than that of a gardener can possibly be."

J. C. LOUDON

"I wish I could in any words paint the hues of these splendid Delphiniums; such shades of melting blue, some light, others dark, some like the summer heaven, and dashed across their pale azure wings with delicious rose."

CELIA THAXTER. AN ISLAND GARDEN 1894

iris   montbretia

granny's bonnet

geranium

old fashioned
pinks

nemesia

foxgloves

lychnis

June 28th

A day out. A summery day - blue skies and warm sunshine. The grass is still a little damp as I sit down to paint - it smells so sweet as it dries. Borders of mixed perennials are woven with colour and texture. Tall spires of kniphofia tilt over sweeps of montbretia. Cushion heads of verbena cast a purple haze, freckled with pale pink geranium. The clip of secateurs and the swish of a rake give away the gardener's pursuits among the azaleas.

"A man cannot be a good gardener, unless he be thoughtful, steady, and industrious: possessing a superior degree of sobriety and moral excellence, as well as genius and knowledge adapted to his business. He should be modest in his manners and opinion." J.C. LOUDON
ENCYCLOPAEDIA OF GARDENING 1871

My brush wavers over the paper
as I contemplate shades of
ultramarine, prussian blue
cyanine blue and violet –
then the sunlight catches
a petal and the palette
at once is suffused with
cobalt turquoise and
cerulean blue.

July

" I know nothing so pleasant
as to sit there on a summer
afternoon, with the western
sun flickering through
the great elder-tree,
and lighting up our
gay parterres, where
flowers and flowering
shrubs are set as
thick as grass in a
field, a wilderness of
blossom, interwoven,
intertwined,
wreathy, garlandy,
profuse beyond
all profusion. "

Mary Mitford
Our Village

8th July – Even in a garden already wallowing in colour, nature herself produces delightful surprises that supersede our best-laid plans. I found a pale blue iris amidst a cloud of faded pink geranium. One bird-sown cerise double poppy, papery feathered petals, new and crumpled.

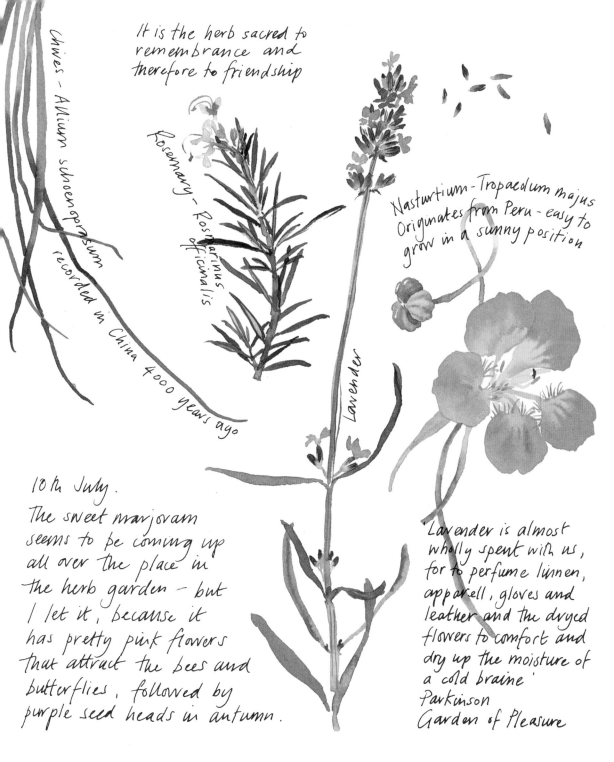

Chives - Allium schoenoprasum recorded in China 4000 years ago

It is the herb sacred to remembrance and therefore to friendship

Rosemary - Rosmarinus officinalis

Nasturtium - Tropaedum majus Originates from Peru - easy to grow in a sunny position

Lavender

10th July.
The sweet marjoram seems to be coming up all over the place in the herb garden – but I let it, because it has pretty pink flowers that attract the bees and butterflies, followed by purple seed heads in autumn.

'Lavender is almost wholly spent with us, for to perfume linnen, apparell, gloves and leather and the dryed flowers to comfort and dry up the moisture of a cold braine'
Parkinson
Garden of Pleasure

mauve
flowers in
midsummer

hang
dried in
bunches

Plant garlic near roses to enhance perfume

herb
butter
for
vegetables

chop in salads

burn
rosemary
stems
for a
lovely
aroma

attract bees

infuse as tea

chop and
sprinkle
over fish

lavender
vinegar

tasted
by
Marco
Polo in
China

pickle
in
vinegar

millstone at the entrance to the herb garden

salad burnet bruised leaves smell like cucumber. russian sage good for stuffing duck, goose and pork. golden marjoram feverfew featherfew, bachelor's buttons, daisy like yellow centred flower. fennel 'we use it to lay upon fish or to boyle it therewith and with divers other things, as also the seeds in bread and other things' Parkinson 1640. rue 'the juice thereof warmed in a pomegranate shell or rind and dropped into the ears helps the pains of them' Culpeper. pink hyssop traditionally used to clean sacred places. evergreen bushy herb native to sonthern europe. wormwood very bitter herb grow near hen houses to deter lice. bistort snakeweed. broad oval leaves with heart shaped base. sweet cicely myrrhis odorata, botanic name derived from greek word for perfume. angelica should flower on the feast day of Archangel Michael. golden sage 'how can a man grow old who has sage in his garden' Chinese proverb. garden catmint attracts bees and cats! beware. rosemary spread linen to dry over a rosemary bush in the sun - the lasting fragrance will repel moths. alecost introduced to America by early settlers who used the fragrant leaves as bookmarks in their bibles. Lavender from the latin 'lavare' to wash, hang a bag of lavender flowers in the flow of water when filling a bath. Valerian grow near vegetables to encourage growth. purple sage soothes the throat

when used in tea. ~~thyme~~ the garden time, to be placed nigh to Bee-hives (for the commodity of honey) Thomas Hyll 1590. ~~white hyssop.~~ pot marjoram ancient culinary herb named by the Greeks - 'joy-of-the-mountain' ~~silver Thyme~~. ~~narrow leaf sage~~ spanish sage, good for teas ~~chamomile~~ chamomile tea for insomnia ~~tansy~~ good antiseptic properties ~~marigold~~ calendula believed to be always in flower on the first day of each month. ~~welsh onion~~ from China and Japan - white flowerhead strong flavoured cylindrical leaves. ~~ ~~ vervain supposed to have originated in Egypt from the 'tears of Isis' ~~blue hyssop~~ loved by bees and butterflies ~~horehound~~ heart shaped, hairy wrinkled leaves, high in vitamin C. ~~Old man~~ Southernwood or wormwood. Its ashes mixed in an ointment will promote the growth of a beard. Women would carry large bunches to church to ward off drowsiness. ~~Lemon balm~~ "An essence of Balm, given every morning will renew youth, strengthen the brain, relieve languishing nature and prevent baldness"
Loudon Dispensary 1696 ~~french sorrel~~ grows in mountainous districts, good for soups ~~cotton lavender~~ or santolina, yellow button like flowers. Place twigs amongst linen to keep the moths away ~~Good King Henry~~ or goosefoot. boil and eat like spinach. also called 'fat hen' after the habit in Germany of feeding it to poultry. ~~lungwort~~ or Jerusalem cowslip, spotted with white, resembling the appearance of lungs. ~~chives~~ chop and mix into the food of newly hatched turkeys.

15th July - Arrived back from holiday intoxicated with impressions of gardens visited, to find my garden tangled with colour

and vigour -
cornflower
potentilla, achillea
scabious, heuchera,
nigella, nasturtium,
viola, poppy, lychnis,
anemone japonica -
marked the best
blooms with coloured
thread as a reminder of which
seeds to collect later in the year.

" Never fail, as you go by, to record what bush is to be moved, and which retained, and which is pretty, and which, on consideration, is held unworthy of too prominent a place "

Reginald Farrer
in a Yorkshire Garden
1909

Cosmos and tobacco plant in the front border.

17th July   Being eight
months pregnant, it is becoming
increasingly difficult to reach that
offending weed, or pick my way to the back
of the border to re-stake the lingering
hollyhocks. I love their fat brown seedheads,
bulging open like a purse full of money.

30th July 6 P.M. I pause to put my feet up on someone else's bench, a fine victorian affair with small wheels at one end for easy manouvering. Positioned at the moment to catch the last of the evening sun. Past low lines of santolina and trimmed lawn, the garden becomes delightfully overgrown. Our legs are teased by broken stems as we linger on the narrow gravel paths. Above the scuffle of our feet on the

stones, I can hear
the leaves of the copper beech
whispering dryly to one another, and the hum of bees,
busy about the sedum. Still blooming, towering heads
of sunflowers in shades from coral to russet. A feathery
bank of cosmos – deep pink, paler and crisp white.
Sweet peas meander along the perimeter of the
vegetable patch. A wall of espalied pears, golden in the
evening sun, hang heavy in the sheltered warmth of
chiselled flint. Apples cluster around twisted boughs,
blackbirds and bees feast on those that have fallen already.

August.

" About the edges of the yellow corn,

And o'er the gardens grown somewhat outworn

The bees went hurrying to fill up their store;

The apple boughs bent over more and more;

With peach and apricot the garden wall

Was odorous, and the pear began to fall

From off the high tree with each freshening breeze."
WILLIAM MORRIS . "AUGUST"   EARTHLY PARADISE 1868-1870

2nd August. Japanese anemones billow in skirts of pink and white, sweetly scented honeysuckle catches the breeze.

"Of all the months in the year this is the one in which the keenest amateur can best afford to leave home, and if I do not go away, it is the one I can best spare to my gardener for his holiday."

MRS C. W. EARLE
POT-POURRI FROM A SURREY GARDEN 1887

A bit of a lull in the garden – an opportune time to give birth!

7th August. Reuben Charles entered the world safely in the midday heat. He has quickly become accustomed to being my garden companion – his pram neatly balancing my drawing board, sketching stool, and jam-jars for water. Parked under a tree he happily applies himself to the subtleties of cedar, oak or ash. Or sleeps.

August 20th
A garden visit – Along blackberry lanes, mixed beech hedges,
old man's beard and bracken. Heavy ripe elderberry heads.
A garden enclosed, an old brick wall, pink and grey,
spotted white with lichen, topped with moss.
An edwardian rockery on a sunny slope – creeping with
Fragaria, scented stocks, burgundy and yellow violas.
Dried marjoram heads, crisp purple brown.
A garden of surprises. An immaculate green croquet
lawn, enveloped by clipped yew, surveyed by two
topiary peacocks. Four wirey lurchers lope nose to tail
through a gateway, ash grey, white, brown and
sandy grey, long claws scrape across the flagstones.
Late summer colour – cosmos, penstemon, cornflower,
and purple asters. Newly planted limes create

an avenue down to a Doric temple. A scarecrow, straw hands and spotted necktie watches over ripe tomatoes. A garden of sounds - droplets from a fountain patter down on the creamy cups of a water lily. Black and white bantams scratch the earth and a peacock lets out a screech from the herbaceous border. A gentle breeze slips through the needles of an ancient cedar - its arms spread wide over the main lawn.

"There is nothing much more difficult to do in outdoor gardening than to plant a mixed border well, and to keep it in beauty through the summer."

GERTRUDE JEKYLL

22nd August. There's no break in the hot dry weather, which means the garden needs regular attention to keep it looking good. As gaps appear in the borders I pop in the odd well-chosen bedding plant to eke out the season. Begonia sempeflorens, with its rusty leaves and showers of white flowers, thrives in the shade of the cistus. A row of pinks spill their spidery limbs over the path. Nicotiana (Havanna Apple Blossom) near the house gives off its sweetest perfume in the evening. Terracotta pots overflow with double deep red geraniums. 23rd August. It's not dark until 10 pm. The warm

evenings are a soothing time – away from the midday
heat, to wander, pockets heavy with twine and secateurs,
snipping dead heads, propping up weary stalks, until
darkness obscures all sensible activity. Fading rose
petals catch the moonlight as they fall.
"No evening scents, I think, have the fascination of
the delicate fragrance of the evening primroses,
especially that of the commonist variety. Those pale
moons irradiate the twilight with their sweet
elusive perfumes. "

ELEANOUR SINCLAIR ROHDE.
THE SCENTED GARDEN

Ageratum Blue champion

alyssum Carpet

Easter bonnet

lobelia

Cambridge blue

String of pearls

Impatiens safari

tempo

orange star

begonia sypeflorens
Ambassador

King Henry

Gold variegated

sage

pyrethrum

golden moss

Purpurea

Clary Sage

23rd
Collected flowers for drying — rosebuds, achillea, larkspur,
hydrangea, nigella seed-pods. Hang upside down in
bunches in a dry dark room.

August 24th. St Bartholomew's Day.
St Bartholomew brings
the cold dew

Nigella damascena,
leave seed pods to self
sow for next year.

plumbago

sow more blue cornflowers next year

too many weeds

saxifrage hiding around

the corner

Anemone
japonica
prefers
partial
shade

fragile angels choir poppy

ddlea to
tract the
tterflies
riegated
th deep
rple
wers.

the cheery face of the viola

do not plant so
many nasturtiums
next year.

Lobelia
Queen Victoria

give the lupins a
dose of soapy water
to get rid of the slugs.

silvery
lamium
leaves for
dark
corners.

vely evening scent
eep crimson, white and
me green.

September

" For those who have not got very good
memories for the names of plants, I
strongly recommend them if they can draw
to make a little coloured sketch, however
small on the page of a gardening book next
the name of the plant. This will be found
a great help to the memory."

Mrs C. W. Earle
Pot-Pourri from a Surrey Garden.
1887.

elderberry

Wild strawberry

Rosa rugosa

Fragaria pink panda

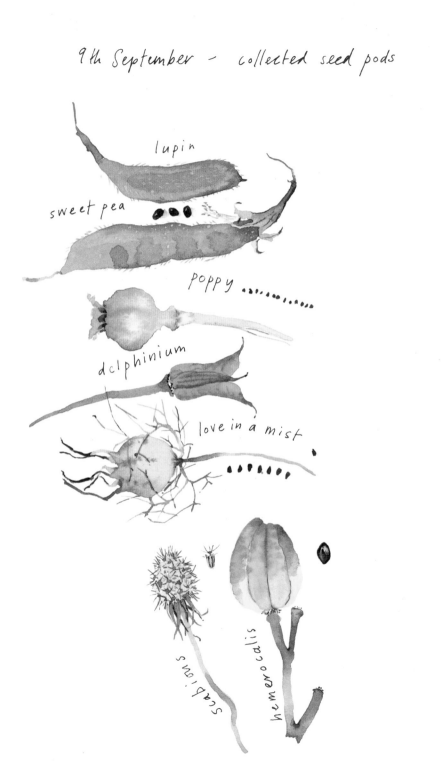

9th September — collected seed pods

lupin

sweet pea

poppy

delphinium

love in a mist

scabious

hemerocalis

Centaurea montana

pot marjoram

rose hips

nicotiana

10 th September - Jobs to be done.....
- tie in new shoots around rose arch while they're still supple.
- take cuttings of non-hardy plants for overwintering - osteospermum, lantana, geranium - leave the geranium cuttings on the potting bench to wilt overnight, They'll strike much better.

14th - Nutting day - the devil will hold the branches down whilst you harvest the nuts.

September 12th. Digging in the garden making space for winter pansies. I unearthed a worm that had tied itself in a knot. I admit I was too squeamish to attempt to unravel it, and left it to its crooked path.

FLOWER SEEDS.

PANSY GIANT MIXED

AVERAGE CONTENTS 100 SEEDS

"There are few things to be done in a garden which do not require a dexterity in operation, and a nicety in hitting the proper season for doing it."
London. Encyclopaedia of Gardening 1871.

gold ochre
persian red
cobalt violet rose
cadmium yellow
burnt umber
french ochre
raw sepia
payne's gray

14th. A breezy day
but beautifully warm. The
soft billowing colours of summer
are giving way to autumn. Silver
grey and dusty brown, alchemilla
heads turned burnt sienna.
Santolina, lavender and lamb's
ears - grey green, brushed

with tall brown spires of salvia. Michaelmas daisies (wild asters) "a symphony in purple, the colour of the organ peal are they" Martha Flint. Golden rod - according to legend grows on the site of buried treasure - arches its feathery heads over the back of the border, while deep yellow rudbeckias light up the front. "The sun has shone on the earth, and the golden rod is his fruit" Thoreau

19th September -
Heard the woodpecker in the tall ash.

21st September -
End of another week of glorious sunshine. The mornings start chilly and the sun hardly rises above the

Nicotiana Havana Appleblossom

Hemerocallis 'Stella d'Oro'

September Charm

Anemone japonica

Scabious

Pansy

Michaelmas Daisy

Catmint

Leospermum 'Giles Gilbey'

Plumbago

...sia Madame Cornelissen

3rd Sept.

tallest treetops, but it throws a lovely
gentle light which doesn't bleach out colours
like the burning summer sun. The catmint,
its flowers scorched and papery white all
summer, now glows an almost luminous
purple in the kind afternoon sun. The
creamy white lantana flowerheads sing
against their deep lush foliage. Growing
through it, the dainty blue star-like
flowers of the plumbago enjoy a new
intensity.

22nd - Planted out wallflowers -
blood red, a good flower early next
year for butterflies. I keep digging
up shiny brown horse chestnuts, newly
tucked underground by the squirrels.
The horse chestnut leaves are beginning
to turn olive and amber.

25th. Still warm and muggy - no rain
for ages. For the first time this
autumn I have crunched freshly fallen
leaves underfoot.

October

"Under the influence of all this loveliness, almost I am persuaded to love autumn best, and forget a lifelong allegiance to the spring-time of the year. Such infidelity could be brought about by nothing less than a month like this, so wondrously, serenely beautiful."
— 11th October, 1899

E. V. BOYLE 'SYLVANA'S LETTERS TO AN UNKNOWN FRIEND'

3rd October. Warm sunshine continues daily - many plants are having a second flush of flowers.

6th October. Our wedding anniversary. Andrew presented me with a cockerel! A delightful life-size rusty iron one. His chosen domain is among the lupins outside the kitchen window. He has quickly become a favourite vantage point for my resident robin redbreast.

7th. Rain at last. Woke this morning to see the soil soaked to a bitter chocolate colour. Fine droplets hang heavy on the   many cobwebs.

Winter weather and women's thoughts often change.

The dimpled leaves of alchemilla mollis each cradle a tiny glistening pool. The japanese anemones sway as naked stalks and the cosmos droop.

8th October. Rain and bluster all day. The dramatic change in the weather is a timely reminder to bring in all my tender plants before the first frosts catch us unawares.

15th. Planting out some rooted lavender cuttings, a young frog surprised and delighted me — quite camouflaged under the mexican orange,

I readily supposed he was busy reducing my slug
population. My weeding companion – a bright eyed
robin followed me closely, enjoying the pickings from
the newly dug earth.
- Always carry a conker in your pocket when digging,
to prevent backache. ANON
17th October. A warmer day but still damp. A
flock of sparrows chattering noisily in the forsythia give
the garden such an air of excitement, I'm almost
inclined to forgive them for stripping the bush of buds
earlier in the year.
Split some perennials that had become overcrowded –
sedum, scabious, stachys. heuchera, and started
enlarging old beds to accomodate them.
"It is a very good plan, when you want to
cut a new bed or alter the shape of an old
one, to shuffle along the wet dewy grass on
an October morning–and this leaves a mark
which enables you very well to judge the size
shape and proportion before you begin to cut

sedum

poppy seed heads

your beds out." MRS C W EARLE. POT-POURRI FROM A SURREY GARDEN
Saved the sedum flower heads (Autumn Joy) still tinged with ruby red but by now quite dry, to combine with jet black birch twigs and poppy seed heads for Christmas wreaths.

18th October - St Luke's day - if it has been a poor summer 'St Lukes little summer' will follow giving a few days of good weather.

20th October - Traditionally the day to prepare mincemeat for Christmas cooking - Chopped apple, raisins, currants, sultanas, suet, brandy.

21st. The first leaves on the japanese cherries are flickering yellow and orange. The flowering plum is fading from deep purple to pinky red - the view through my studio windows is becoming a completely new palette.

25th. First overnight frosts of the year. The begonias I hadn't already brought indoors, to flower on the kitchen windowsill, have been turned to a pulp.

birch twigs

raffia

elderberry

honeysuckle

honeysuckle

holly

hawthorn

November

Sorbus

yew

honeysuckle

pyracantha

bacciflava

"The garden is never dead; growth is always going on and growth that can be seen, and seen with delight.

CANON H. ELLACOMBE 'IN MY VICARAGE GARDEN AND ELSEWHERE' 1901

November 2nd – Found violets blooming amongst the irises – folklore would have it that an autumn flowering violet will send the landowner to his grave. I prefer to think of it as

grackle

Maidens name your chestnuts true, the first to burst belongs to you.

willow

honesty

unearthing a jewel on a grey day. The horse chestnut is the first to lose all its leaves.

November 8th – Damp mild day – perfect for an autumn clean up. Save the ash from bonfires to spread around your fruit trees. The last few leaves are clinging stoically to the cherry branches - the ground beneath is an unruffled blanket of orange and red. I will enjoy the richness of nature's canvas for a couple of days before desecrating it with my rake.

lime

11th Nov. St Martin's Day
The first day of
winter.

snowberry

hydrangea petiolaris

Rosa rugosa

Lonicera fragrantissima

There have been certain colours this autumn that will remain in my memory - chartreuse leaves edged with burgundy - one day I'll create a new border based on this combination. Yellow maple leaves with bright red stalks.

November 18th. An extremely windy night followed by a pinty orange sunrise – and then heavy rain. The last few chrysanthemums are bowing sodden heads. Broken twigs lay scribbled over the lawn,

and the last few leaves have been tossed and discarded by the wind. The whole garden has assumed an air of melancholy.
"Sharpen and mend tools, gather oziers and hassell rods and make baskets in stormy weather"
                                                                        1727

"One of the most disagreeable months...but he may console himself with the shortness of the day, and hail the approach of evenings when he may cast aside his wet dress and fortify his mind by converse with books."
J.C. Loudon Encyclopaedia of Gardening 1882

"footnote"

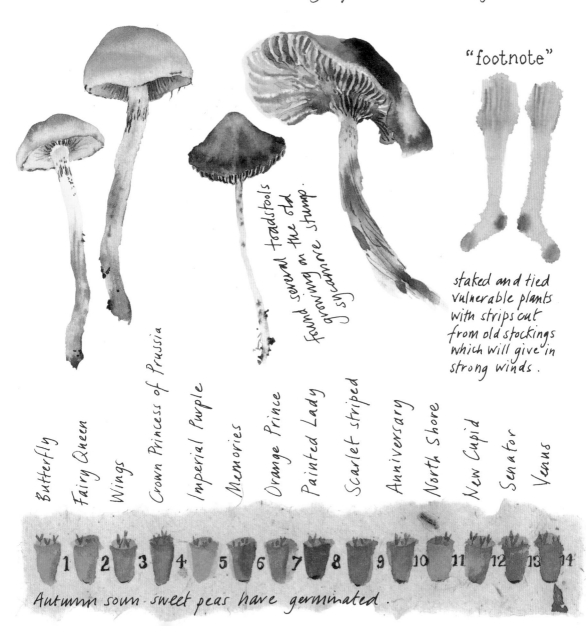

found several toadstools growing on the old sycamore stump.

staked and tied vulnerable plants with strips cut from old stockings which will give in strong winds.

Butterfly

Fairy Queen

Wings

Crown Princess of Prussia

Imperial Purple

Memories

Orange Prince

Painted Lady

Scarlet striped

Anniversary

North Shore

New Cupid

Senator

Venus

1 2 3 4 5 6 7 8 9 10 11 12 13 14

Autumn sown sweet peas have germinated.

November 19th

Noticed the first flower on the winter
jasmine — an invaluable shrub that will
thrive in the most unpromising of places and flower resolutely
throughout winter. I will be raiding it regularly along with
lonicera fragrantissima for indoor arrangements. The former
for it's cheerful yellow face, the latter for it's lemony fragrance.
A tall unidentified rose needs more support — so I set about
twisting sticks and twine to make an obelisk.

20th — St Edmund's Day — patron saint of gardeners and
farmers. Gathered a posy of flowers from the garden in his
honour.

"Set garlicke and pease
St Edmund to please"

Planted a few garlic
cloves near the roses to
repel aphids.
November 22nd All the leaves
have fallen off the forsythia
revealing a ragged sparrow's nest
entwined in its branches. Inside
an abandoned silver grey
snail shell looks strangely
egg like.

Cut some long flexible twigs
off the bush - wrapped them
around and around securing now
and again with raffia to make
a sphere for the top of
my rose obelisk.

29th November – Planted a chorus of
winter pansies to sing against grey skies.
'Everything is good in its season.' Italian Proverb.

" Even deep snow gives time for cleaning, thrashing and sorting

December

seeds, preparing

stakes and pea-sticks,

tying mats,

sorting bulbs."

J.C. LOUDON

Topiary Figures

The Red Dragon of Wales

The Lion of England

The Greyhound of Richmond

The Black Bull of Clarence

2nd December. Snow overnight - the first this winter. In the morning I went round brushing snow off the shrubs - most had been flattened to half their height and sprang back thankfully when I shook them.
It's getting dark by 4pm. Frosts are forecast for the week.
8th December. Bright sunny and blustery, squirrels are busy foraging and digging. Potted a final few bulbs - an irresistible bargain bag of tulips, iris and crocus - only spring

will reveal the secret of their colours. Covered
the pots with netting to keep the squirrels out.
16th December. Coldest day we've had so far. A sharp
wind and those heavy skies that promise snow.
Later in the afternoon tiny flakes skate horizontally
past my windows. The light covering of snow highlights
the value of evergreens, to give shape and structure
to the garden in winter.

The Griffin

The White Lion
of Mortimer

The Falcon of the Plantagenets.

'A hedge between keeps friendships green.

"God Almightie first Planted
a Garden. And indeed it is
the Purest of Humane pleasures.
It is the Greatest Refreshment
to the Spirits of Man; I doe
hold it, there ought to be
Gardens for all the Moneths
in the Yeare; In which, severally,
things of Beautie may be then
in season. For December you
must take such Things as are
Greene all Winter; Holly; Ivy;
Bayes; Juniper; Cipresse Trees;
Eugh; Pine-Apple-Trees; Firre-
Trees; Rose-Mary; Lavander;
Periwinckle; the White, the
Purple, and the Bleue; Germander;
Flagges; Orenge-Trees; Limon-
Trees; And Mirtles, if they be
stooved; and Sweet Mariorum,
warme set."

FRANCIS BACON. ESSAYES 1597

18th December.
Gathered holly and ivy for
making christmas garlands —
the blackbirds have already
stolen all the holly berries.
Where space allows I have
delayed cutting down some
perennials that offer more
interest than the naked earth.
The brittle bleached flower stalks
of hemerocallis fan out in front
of an arching fern.
21st December —
St Thomas's day — the shortest
day — it's now dark by 3.30 pm.
Made christmas pot-pourri —
dried orange slices, dried
lemon peel, cinnamon sticks,
cloves, star anise, bay leaves,
small fir cones.

24th December.
Christmas Eve - Girls who want to conjure
up an image of their partner-to-be
should walk backwards, nine
times around a pear tree.

December 25th Christmas Day –

Unfortunately a rather wet and dreary day outside. When I looked out this morning two fine lady hens had joined my cockerel in the lupins —

Thankyou Andrew!

"of statues, busts, pedestals, altars, urns and similar sculptures. Used sparingly, they excite interest, often produce character and are always individually beautiful." J.C. LOUDON. ENCYCLOPAEDIA OF GARDENING 1871.

Helleborus foetidus.
Dec 80.

"I want it said by those who know me
best, that I always plucked a thistle
and planted a flower where I
thought a flower would
grow." ABRAHAM LINCOLN

Biographical notes:

E.V. Boyle 1825–1916 'Sylvana's letter to an unknown friend' 1900.
Wrote and illustrated books about the garden she
restored at Huntercombe Manor, Buckinghamshire.

Henry Arthur Bright. 1830–1884. 'A year in a Lancashire garden' 1879.
Partner in a shipping firm, also cultivated his
own garden in Lancashire, about which he
wrote and published his diaries.

Mrs C.W. Earle. 1836–1925. 'Pot-pourri from a Surrey garden' 1887.
Studied at South Kensington School of Art before
becoming a gardener, writer, wife and mother. She
established her own garden – 'Woodlands' in
Cobham, Surrey, and wrote extensively about it
and contemporary issues, in her diaries. She
published these, ignoring derisory comments from
her husband and they became immediate
bestsellers.

John Gerard 1545–1612. 'Herballe' 1597.
Elizabethan botanist. Published the first detailed
catalogue of plants in any single garden, based
on his own garden in Holborn, London.

Thomas Hyll. 1529–? 'The Gardener's Labyrinth' 1572. (Published
under the pseudonym Didymus Mountain).

Thomas Hyll cont...d. First english-language popular gardening manual to be published, which included many new plants that were being introduced into Elizabethan England by the explorers. Also published books on astrology, cooking, popular medicine, and psychology.

Thomas Jefferson. 1743-1826. 'Jefferson's Garden Book'. American president and gardening enthusiast. Wrote extensive diaries and correspondence cataloguing his horticultural exploits.

J. C. Loudon. 1783-1843. 'Encyclopaedia of Gardening' 1871. Horticultural editor, writer and traveller. His terraced garden in Gravesend, Kent, could be classed as the first public park. He also designed cemeteries, and proposed a greenbelt for London.

Jane Loudon. 1807-1858. 'Instructions in Gardening for Ladies' 1840. Married J. C. Loudon in 1830. Travelled with her husband and wrote popular horticultural books as a commercial exercise to pay off his debts!

Mary Russell Mitford 1787-1855 'Our Village' 1824-32
Lived with her father near Reading, England and
wrote about gardening to support them both.

Vita Sackville-West (Hon) 1892-1962. A talented novelist and poet
who also wrote a gardening column for
the Observer newspaper for 25 years.
She became best known however for
her garden at Sissinghurst, Kent,
which she created with her husband
Harold Nicolson.

Henry David Thoreau 1817-1862 'The Writings of Henry David
Thoreau'
American naturalist and writer who kept
extensive journals of the habitat around
his home at Waldon Pond.

Louise Beebe Wilder 1878-1938 'Colour in my Garden.' 1927
Grew up in Baltimore and became one of
America's best known and authoritative garden
writers.

salvia nemerosa

iris

Pyrethrum thomasinii

astrantia graniolica

genm
Lady Stratheden

veronica sightseein

alchemilla mollis

papaver orientale
harvest moon

lupin